Fine Lines

Fine Lines

Carol Burnes

HEADLAND

For Henry Walden, who took a chance on a poet

Copyright 1992 by Carol Burnes

Full CIP is available for this book from The British Library.

ISBN 0 903074 64 8

First Published in 1992 by HEADLAND PUBLICATIONS

38 York Avenue
West Kirby,
Wirral
Merseyside L48 3JF

ACKNOWLEDGEMENTS

Acknowledgements are due to the editors of the following publications in which some of these poems first appeared (sometimes in slightly different versions): *Anthology of Magazine Verse Yearbook of American Poetry, The Christian Science Monitor, Gargoyle, The Leaflet; NERA Journal, The Little Magazine, The Thread Unbroken; A Quilter's Anthology, 13th Moon, Perspectives on a Grafted Tree, Soundings, Soundings East, Rhino.* "On Leaving", "Long-Distance", and "Cocktail Party" first appeared in the chapbook, *Roots and Wings.*

Special thanks to Mary Swope, a true reveler,
for her editorial guidance in all things.
Special thanks also to Josie Merck for her cover illustration,
to Alison Webber-Cassese for cover design and design consultation.
Thanks!?! to FN Wombat for teaching me the restraint of punctuation!?!!
For typesetting and consultation thanks to The Center for Advanced
Research in Oppressive Binarisms, Cambridge, MA,
Charles Fulton and Sylvia Math.

*Writing poetry is like dancing
in a field of nettles
with no clothes on.*
—Jamie Burnes

CONTENTS

In Search of a New Season

Through the Window

Circles

In Search of a New Season

FINE LINES

Lost beneath a plexiglass sky
she sees a slice of herself
wandering among strangers who stare into glass,
peering beyond their own reflections.
She sees herself repeated. Watching
two young children, girl and boy,
bob after their mother
like bright balloons on tight strings,
she knows the longing for a moment of peace,
knows too, how soon the children are gone.

She enters the bright lit cave
crammed with colors, signs –
the plastic flash and click of dollars spent.
Tunneling through manmade light
where air is synthetic, earth and sky are lost,
she forgets the children.
She sees herself mirrored. Ageless.
Ageing. Fine lines. Searching,
she gathers armloads of who she might be
and in the fitting room, blinking
against bright lights, she strips down,
yearning for a new season.

There is no hiding here.
Who am I? For whom do I dress?
She masquerades her options:
I could be... I could be... Couldn't I?
In mirrors she gleams, crowded by women
shedding used skins, sloughing off
old selves, dry, transparent; fragile
as love. She thinks of the children grown
and the empty shell of herself,
already past wishing to be that young again.

3

And around her the dying.
How we bury who once we were,
grand-daughter, daughter, niece, friend;
they leave us and we become them.
Can she bear to be the elder, parent,
and never the child again?
What is my name – should I keep it?
She tries some on for a closer fit and
in the mirror her face beckons. She thinks
she sees a friend shining darkly,
gleaming, but cold, cold to the touch.
She merges with staring women and winter skin.

Can she bear the silence of old timbers
and empty rooms, of bicycles stacked inside
and the silent stares of teddy bears?
Dust gathers in the doll house
and tiny embroidered mice
no longer dance and stir;
soldiers years ago gave up the march.
What holds her now? This gathering of years?

Before the mirror she slips
into another silken wish;
but not for children.
She fingers the hemmed edge,
the seamed definition,
observes the material shape and flow
of her whole life and sees a new grace;
she feels the smooth possibility
presented in the glass,
and something wild in her burns.

WITHOUT KNOCKING

Without knocking
the sun comes in
strides across the floor
and calls my name

It climbs to find me
reaches into small cold corners
where it hasn't recently been
and doesn't explain

It flashes on every hair
shows me new patterns
in old places
slides across me

everywhere amber
face   hands   hips

AFTER

Folded
into each other
in this dark cocoon
your length fitted to mine
so close I can't feel you from me,
so still I barely sense your silent touch
(how your fingers web my skin)
together we float and drift.
In dim curtained light
even minutes stop.
All the work, lists,
appointments,
calls
lie abandoned in heaps
on the floor with our clothes.
In the warm circle of your arms, I
am safe, held as if now were forever
and the future never a question.
Silent now the voices
that slice and shred,
that nag and warn
as sleep sways us,
holds us gentle
before this day
bursts open,
flings us
shivering
far, far
apart.

FINGER PAINTING

Smooth cool stuff
squeezes between my fingers
Lumps slip and spread
The shudder at my back familiar –
and that old voice says
DON'T

With red and yellow I mix
flame the color of burning
With yellow and blue mix
water, dive in
Across whole walls my hands blaze –
sweep horizons
Landscapes leap from my fingers
and the wall sings
A sun, wide-eyed
watches the mountain rear itself –
Field   Ocean   Sky
I paint the big things

But over my head always
those dark wings beat
Shadows bite and block my vision
I palm the paint to the wall
See what colors do to each other –
Precious   Golden   Darker

AUTOBIOGRAPHICAL NOTES

I weave webs to draw people in,
have many friends, but never enough
and sometimes lose their names.
I spin gossamar thread
as if I could patch the dream,
but seldom remember my dreams.
Some days even daylight is a question,
I cling to my small black twist of doubt.
Voices warn me awake –
there is no tomorrow.
Listen.

Leaving is forever,
and I hate doors closed.
I collect keys that unlock nothing,
petals crumbling to the slightest touch,
the feathered plumes of times past.
Carefully I stitch each one
tightly, precisely in.
I hoard old clothes, books, ticket stubs,
small notes, you;
your voice all around me,
your words as if they could save me –
repeat, repeat.

I fill the freezer against
some barren time
when all growing stops

and I must grope
in the icy chamber
to find some small package
wrapped and sealed,
frozen hard as stone;

put there in the green time,
stored against the ache, the cold.

BIG BLUE

It seems my father's big blue four door
Chrysler 'seventy-five station wagon
with scratches and vague dents
that mostly he put in, forgetting
the hand brake or scraping his own garage door
(he would have yelled at us for less)
is always parked in the same place
in Mother's front yard, give or take a few feet,
shimmering steely blue, forever
like his eyes, like mine too,
even seven years now since he died.

Blue is part of the landscape, waiting there
like the stones that edge the unruly lawn
beneath the huge oak whose lazy, leafy arms
drop acorns clapping against the smooth roof,
a sign of early fall or harsh winter;
Blue, vaguely reflecting the passers-by
though yearly the shine dims down.
Big Blue shimmies now as it drives,
floats along the road with the drift and sway
of a huge sleepy cloud, so
today Mother is giving Big Blue away.

She hands them papers, and passing by
I see the heavy door open, waiting
for another life, and glimpse the pale blue
stuffed leather seats we all crowded into
while he drove us around
to the stench of his slow cigar,
and on the dash board, small supplies
of cough drops, chewing gum, loose change.

I used to watch for Big Blue,
the familiar slam of the door, and sneak
to see his face, discover his mood –
sometimes brooding, heavy and dark,
the storm about to break as he lashed out
at one of us kids for nothing we could name,
raging attack on someone.
Those thunderous days
I learned to say little, ask nothing, hide.
Other days he shone from the car,
the sky in his eyes, playful,
his arms an open greeting,
(oh how he played with us then)
tumbled us with hugs, telling stories
about Leo the Lion. He'd snarl and roar
while I sucked the Vicks cough drops
both of us ate like candy.

There was no one sillier than my father.
He could suck in his breath and almost drop his pants
like Charlie Chaplin, or do Bob Hope
and show us the sexy slidey step
across the floor we never learned.
He put on hats and acted out each one
while we laughed until we cried.
All my way through school and college
he drew us in with stories and sage advice
so friends would gather and stay, some
claiming him more father than their own.

He always went to work in that car
or one just like it, wearing a brown felt hat
that soon enough someone sat on.
Whenever I tried to imagine God,

I knew He wore a hat like that.
Now I see Big Blue, the metallic gleam grown dull,
a silhouette known so deeply
there's no need for details of eyes or face
and I feel the words we never said.
I imagine Blue sliding away with cigar smoke,
the endless stories and his wisdom hidden inside,
the old engine humming familiar as life, but dimmer,
dimmer, receding down the road.

This morning my son, cleaning out the car,
found six cigars and sadly brought them to me.
Suddenly I saw Father, clear as the day
before he died, driving by my house
in his faded yellow floppy brimmed hat
and the gun-metal blue sweater he always wore,
his smooth, gentle hands on the wheel,
and the shine in his eyes.

In the turn of a key
a spark catches;
an engine roars to life.

HOUSE PLANTS

I run a greenhouse, a shelter
for awkward, unwanted wanderers –
it's spring inside year round.
Even in the lean of winter
they spew green and flourish.
They pry at windows, crowd the corners,
branch and tangle overhead
from walls and beams, demanding, strident.
I feed them.
I shift them to find the right light,
comfort, advise, listen
and listen.

But they burst their pots, grow
gangly limbs that sprawl and cling
to snag my passing.
They leaf out the sun,
their thirst is endless,
their silent growth exhausts me.

At night in the quiet of sleeping
I know I hear leaves turn,
stems tremble,
as they shift and plot
to clamber from their pots,
uproot
and run their green rebellion
through my bed.

LONG-DISTANCE

I have these words you sent me,
strong and reassuring on the page,
but I want your voice,
the touch of your hand.
Days I find myself stopped
thinking of you;
what I would say,
how you would listen,
how together we would celebrate
each word,
each green blade.

Today I woke up thinking
maybe, if I open one eye slowly,
I'll find you beside me.
I look at the big towel by the shower,
the one you used
that would fit around us both,
and I see you standing naked,
waiting.

I close my eyes to remember
your voice,
soft as the shade of hemlocks
woven overhead;
your touch,
little fingers of rain,
the steady gentle sound of it,
of breathing,
of leaves;
the long, deep shiver.

HALLOWEEN SONNET

Today, my dear, my demons are out, flapping
ragged around this room, but you can't seem
to see their flashing shadows, biting wings.
You see only me locked in my waking dream,
living it out. "Cinema of the skull," you say
and go about the business of leaving. You tie
your tie, smooth each hair, nothing stray,
no sign of strain in your appearance. Then my
voices hiss, "Do not believe," to each
soft thing you say. Against you, demons hold
me stiff and choke me with the wild-eyed speech
I fling in your calm face. You firmly fold
me burning, close; your feelings safely glassed
and hidden, you assume all demons pass.

KEEPING

With careful fingers
stitching soft cloth, she quilts her own legend,
her life a patchwork of bright, small pieces
fitted tightly, sewn and knotted in.
More intricate than snowflakes,
than feathered wings,
her visions, her voices, her new loves;
dreams unfurl like sails
to catch and hold the wind.
Hands never empty, never still,
needle flying, she
fastens everything in:
how at night the sky falls
softly in a field full of thistle
tufted the color of moon;
how finches, yellow and darting,
gather seeds,
and for their nests collect
only the softest stuff.
All she treasures
she keeps.
In the foothills a secret city
unfolds, tucked between rock and tree,
new snow sugaring slanted roofs.
Seeing the blood of swamp maples rise,
water swirl over rocks
eddying whispers,
she stitches.

Finding scraps of blue
in a box,
she sees the whole horizon
and with quick strong fingers,
firmly sews in sky.

ENGRAVING
for my aunt

Passing the old engraving, grey traced on grey,
hung on the bedroom wall where I grew up –
the room once my room, I never look for long.
In the print, a small wire-haired dog waits,
legs braced, head down, staring
at the freshly dug mound
of dirt heaped over the hole
where last he saw his master
lowered into the ground.
Days and nights alone he shivers
and waits, framed on the wall.
I know. I watch.

I wait too.
When they told me she'd killed herself
right next door while I was sleeping,
I was standing in the barn stroking her old horse –
the one she taught me to ride on,
leading me through leafy dreams,
showing me the secrets of the woods;
year after year we rode the seasons together.
Silence settled around me thick as fog
and in the trees birds froze
with songs stuck in their throats.
The sun, hanging over the hill,
could not move.

When they buried her
I watched,
heard the words,
sang the songs,
heard the dirt hit
hard wood
and waited.

Months I waited, until one morning
they put her old horse down
after I'd polished her one last time,
feeding her carrots and promises,
telling her it would be all right.
All the while the machine dug and snarled
into darkness, tearing new grass and earth.
I handed her over to strangers, watched them
lead her away to the upper field
on a long green path of sun.
She shone like new pennies,
swinging her head and tail side to side,
her long easy strides following, free –
so glad to go for new grass again.
They led her between mounds
of fresh earth heaped, and torn roots
with stones upturned, glaring,
to the edge of a dark hole
where it took four shots.

Smashing across the field
I heard them –

shot upon
shot.
It was as though
I held the gun
and knew then
exactly how
her soft dark eyes
rolled white,
her knees trembled,
folded
as she went down.

Across green fields
I bless her still
and wait.

EXECUTION

Today is the killing day as planned.
The hole is dug on schedule.
I take her for grass one last time
before they shoot her.
She leaps free –
I grab for her lead and miss.
Streaking devil, shining black
ebony hurtling across the field
black hooves cutting soft green
black tail pluming death
she runs
wheels and rears
gallops near
to lunge at me, all teeth
bone hard clamping, white teeth snapping shut.
She spins, lashes out barely missing my head –
a deep horse scream stuck in her throat.
She tosses her mane, a raging wave of black.

Run Annie run for your life...
Here Annie come get grain.

Still as stone she stands gleaming
the rich smell of grain compels
the rattle of grain in a pail pulls her.
She swings her head then takes a step near
eyes flashing, white stars
head high, ears working –
she can't decide.
She's black and still and free.
On her arched chest sweat glistens
her smooth flanks heave.

Run Annie run for your life...
Here Annie have some oats.
Come girl have some oats.
Run Annie run for your life....

Life is a bullet in the head.

IN SEARCH OF A NEW SEASON

Silently watching the grey ends
of bushes and trees,
she waits for new growth,
for buds, still hard knots,
to loosen.

She'll feel it before she sees it,
when the ground gives to her feet
and the wind no longer whips her
but funnels gently past,
tearing and scattering clouds.

Her head will fill with flowers
before the field does,
and when the crocus shoves up
yellow as yolk,
she, hungry for new growing things,
will stand ready to fork it.

Through the Window

MACHINING

Hovered over the sewing machine,
a waterfall of cloth tumbling down her lap,
she leaned into stitches,
the silver needle piercing, piercing.
Every day after school I found her
lost among crinkly paper patterns,
Vogue magazines stacked high,
the measuring tape snaking across cloth,
and pins in the old filigreed silver soap box,
walls of material piled, silent, around her.

I glimpsed rainbows of thread in drawers
with chalks she used to measure and mark.
I heard the pinking shears grind as
cut pieces fell. Mirrors and fittings,
she draped the mannequin's pale plaster body
with dreams of peau de soie, chiffon,
taffeta and voile, viyella and fine cotton.
Pinning, unpinning, shifting filmy patterns,
shaping dreams, she fitted cloth to every vision;
while over the voice of the machine I talked.

To her bent head, to her back I talked,
I scattered my day around her in pieces.
Over her shoulders I showered words
while she machined.
As she basted and button-holed, stitched
and trimmed, I fastened her in with words.
I flew at her with words,
hurled them at the back of her head
while she ran off endless perfect seams
to the whir and purr of her machine.

Over its hum I marked her.
I taped, measured, pinned and cut deep.
I needled her – running stitch, feather stitch,
cross stitch – tried them all.
I doubled the thread, knotted both ends
and sewed words in.
Once with words I drove her to tears
while she, with strong unflinching fingers
and one gold thimble dimpled at the end,
directed unruly cloth beneath the flashing foot,
endless edges perfectly paired,
and the headless torso turned to fittings.

Now, bent to my typewriter,
I machine.
I stitch words to the page in patterns,
embroider dreams
while papers pile and shift,
pencils and pens scatter with books,
and paper clips star against old wood.
Words evenly seam page after page
while I measure visions,
cut and pin each into place.

They snarl and tangle like her thread
and like the needle, pierce through, silver.
Margins fray, edges unravel,
and ends need hemming.
Words stream and stutter, letters tap
while I finger each into place.
And over that hum a soft-voiced "Mommy, Mommy"
shreds my vision, tearing through again;

and some lines later
I turn my head.

WHEN ADA DIES

The long trek ends.
How many thousand miles
did she travel
around this house
taking care of us all?
Now in the empty kitchen,
the fire in the coal stove's often out,
the kettle in the wrong place.
No one puts flowers in our rooms,
tucks hot water bottles between icy sheets;
edges fray and no one mends.
There's a scattering in this house,
a sharp wind blowing through
shifting us all apart,
a draft of cold never here before.
Still her touch lingers, her voice in whispers –
how long before an echo fades, a dream wears off?

Long ago she taught us
to say goodnight, let go.
When the lamp switched off
and the room pitched into darkness
she told us, "Slowly,
slowly eyes grow accustomed,
and even blackness takes on light."

AT FATHER'S FUNERAL

Hands empty
space the color of ice breaking apart
streaks of silver shooting
comets across dark velvet.
Father's white hair, grey blue eyes laughing
everything moving, shifting.

At the graveside the minister, old friend,
stumbles, saying the wrong name –
how Father would have laughed.
The small grey box next to a black hole
beside the careful, cut square of grass –
how small he is now.

Piper on a moss green hill between dark trunks
pipes "Amazing Grace", a deep fierce crying.
Cousin Mary holding bright field flowers,
crimson, blue, white stars in her hands.
Great Aunt looking down, forever, frail
as an orchid, dry face years past crying.

Linking arms to the children's,
I try to catch their grief in my hands,
keep it from them.
Mother, silver grey and bent now,
nearer than ever before.
Soft sobbing, water rising all around me
slipping through my fingers
slivers of silver, prisms I cannot catch.

In the church shoulder to shoulder,
stand up, sit down.
Minister's voice catching,
wanders through his own words.
Leaving, I walk down a long pale corridor
of blue-grey light.

The wail of the bagpipe unwinding overhead –
Father would have liked that.
Holding my head high, wearing blue –
his favorite color.
Faces, pale moons, no names –
I can't find yours.

Outside, standing in sudden sun
smiling, greeting crying people
telling them it will be all right
shaking damp hands
hundreds of hands letting go.
Across a tide of rising faces
your eyes meet mine:
something at last to hold.

MOTHER, AFTER THE FUNERAL

Like this elm
you stand now, stripped,
a network of bare branches and countless twigs
draped, airy like Venetian lace,
a bridal veil of grey smoke
fine as hair, silent as fog.
So you float, the silvery mist
of one breath blown into still air.
All the delicate limbs of your life hang down.
Your strong trunk rooted deep, reaches up;
you do not bend but sway just slightly
in high winds and storm, the bite of winter.
You wait out the deepest waking sleep
that holds all the dying,
and we gather round.
Whatever passes of ice and tears
you catch and keep,
etched silver, white with the season.
In your smooth cool skin of winter,
you rise into a sky of ice,
grey on grey, alone.

ON LEAVING

When you leave
I am left
Holding space,
Your impression in me
Like the hollow
A thumb leaves in clay.

DAYBREAK
as he sees it

I want you, only you are still asleep.
How you waste morning, eyes tightly shut.
I lie here just barely awake
watching grey light filter across the field;
the trees, a wall of black, begin to show
one by one, as daylight dusts their tops,
and pale sunlight claims them.

I watch the fox jump on the hill, a copper flash,
and hear the woodpecker's
tap-tapping on the metal fence.
I'd like to touch you, draw you
into this slow spreading light.
I can take a deep breath now,
feel a stillness before the storm.

The storm begins at seven, shoving
myself into a suit, racing to hay the horses,
make the train. It howls all day,
all week the frenzy of city business,
leaving me only the ends of days and weeks.
I can't bank and farm and build all at once;
beneath the millstone I turn and turn,
whole seasons ground down to dust.

Sometimes at the end of day,
in the final flickering light,
I sit on the wall and watch the sun settle
into the open arms of three sturdy pines;
it sinks down branch by branch –
looks so easy.

ADOPTION
for Sarah

It happened overnight
with a phone call,
you became a mother
and one year later mother again;
like driving into a wall,
your whole life as you'd known it
stopped.

Interviewed, counseled,
you filled out forms
and went through more than most of us;
but you missed that slow
growing wonder,
that folding into yourself
quiet as never before.

Now you grow sparse, leggy.
They flourish
and with small hands
twist your life to fragments;
you are never alone,
can't turn your back –
they're too small.
You bend to chores and long for naps
while they drain
time and attention like milk;
they're so hungry.

You had no idea about the crying:
at night, usually your daughter
wails across your dreams,
and alone in the dark,
half awake, pale in your nightgown,
you go to her.
You grab her, squeeze,
try to shake out the crying,
the dark need
that tangles
your long black hair.

THEY SAY

At school they say you have trouble
learning to read, make letters,
but they should see you now
bent over paper at the kitchen table
clutching a pencil, writing, writing.
Your pony tails curve across each cheek,
two crescents of gold.
Around you candles flicker while
the pencil-shadow dances on the page.
You say: Turn off the lights.
Turn on music!
You nod your head to keep time,
saying words over
in a soft low voice,
choosing the right ones,
drawing each one carefully out
between blue lines.
Your eyes are wide –
you get ahead of yourself.

The words fly out,
flock across the page
flapping,
all eager feathers and wings.

REFLECTIONS

Crystal prisms swing in slivered sunlight
as rainbows scatter
fragments of flame,
smooth ice carves its message.
Pieces of life shatter,
fern fronds
and gold embossed leather,
ageless words bound and shelved,
a story without end.
Eyes peer back,
I repeat myself.

An old woman, too thin
to raise herself, lies lost in pillows,
head turning side to side,
eyes scanning
settle nowhere.
Caged without a song,
she mouths the past,
grasps for words long gone.
Words, her bridge to the world, collapsed:
open, close, open, tongue wagging,
only throat sounds.
Who hears her now,
who pleads her cause?
Her hands close on nothing.
She cannot remember.

Some years ago thick fog
began to fill her,
days lost definition.
Musician, she forgot the music,
lost the song.
She clung to each small thing remembered;

a date, a meal, a trip to the store,
hoarded, polished again like lucky stones.
Finally, in her own house everything turned
strange, "Where am I ?
Where am I?" she called a friend to ask.

Lost in the tangle of time and sheets
she smells the darkness; sight, sound,
taste and touch float and disconnect.
Her son beside her –
who is he?
Her daughter's soft song –
have I heard this before?
Hands from nowhere stroking,
and a spoon of soup, mean nothing,
just snatches of light and flicks of sound.

Her whole life is ragged silk
shredded beyond repair;
the green frond,
the golden word,
lost in a prism of ice
reflecting.

I DREAMED FATHER

I dreamed that my father,
sun streaming from his white hair
and eyes smiling blue sky,
walked across green,
reached his hand to the round brass knob
on my front door, opened it and entered,
as if after four years
he were expected still.
I felt him in my house like an embrace
and asked, was he real,
but he did not answer.

There were people,
shifting between tall green plants
and patches of sun that spilled
through walls of glass,
murmuring,
their voices cresting waves
of sound not unlike music.
Someone served them food,
and there was laughing
and everywhere the simple sound
of father's voice.
Perhaps I moved among people
also offering something,
holding in my hands a polished tray
smooth as the moon,
casting silver images
wherever I went.

There was the glint of crystal,
and somewhere, just over there,
my father's voice, and around him
in gentle rolling swells of light,
the laughing.
I asked again, "Are you real?
Will you stay?"

He smiled as if
there were no answer,
and his smile was enough.
Perhaps he only returned
to story us,
to gather us once again with his words
the way he always did,
and hold us in the telling,
lift us in the sudden wild flight
of all he imagined.
And always the laughing.

He filled my house with his voice,
his vision, pale blue light
rollicking through the rafters,
glowing like moonstones.
And soon there were no questions,
no more wondering why and if,
nor for how long.

THROUGH THE WINDOW

She sees the sun rise from the ocean,
Sit like an orange on the grey ledge
As the beach stretches white, new linen,
Glaring.

Waves roll in, roll out,
Relentless.
Leaving froth, tossing shells,
Sand shifts new layers all night.

Nothing is the same, save
The apple on her window sill,
Still round and green –
All that is left.

Already the new day's blinding heat
Presses her into the sheets.
And on her window
Silver spreads
Grey despair.

Circles

DILEMMA

Rita has been going to the same shrink
for two, three, maybe ten years.
She says he helps.
Though he seldom speaks,
he nods, tips his head,
shifts fingers on his chin
or drums them.

In the deep leather chair
that tips and swivels
made of soft skin,
he leans back.
She's sure he listens;
he blinks.

While she spews her life out,
hoses him,
he says nothing.
Like a witch she conjures him:
Mother, Father, Lover, Everyone
she ever loved or hated
or wished.

Her whole life pours
like fine wine into crystal
while he sniffs and savors,
drinks it slowly down.
Nothing is left
but the silt of years.

Still she has trouble
prying herself from bed,
making friends, leaving the house,
doesn't trust the children,
loves the same man
who loves her and leaves her
again and again.

In silent eyes she sees herself
repeated; mirrored like a tree
on a glassy lake, each limb, each leaf
perfect, though upside down.
Sometimes she too says nothing
but listens to him listen.

RITA, HAS YOUR MAN YET SAID ?

Has he said yet,
"This may blow you away
but you're all I ever wanted in a woman?"
Has he started raving
about how much he loves you,
needs you,
wants you, but
just a little different?
Some small shape of you
doesn't fit him
and you should change.

Does he stand there, just out of reach
and tell you about support,
how you both need it,
and space,
how he needs it -
you the fixed point
while he keeps moving?

While he ties you down
adoring,
has he told you about his wings?
You, almost perfect,
must never expect too much.

And when he's done yelling
and you still sob,
does he wrap himself around you,
hold you close, hang on hard and expect
to stop it all with a kiss?

WHEN THEY ENTER

When they enter your body it's different.
You let them and
they think it gives them rights
like signing contracts or
holding title.
What they use they think they own
like the car
which they always expect
to start right up,
run smoothly,
get them where they're going
and back again.
But when it stops being brand new
they drive it less,
park it more.

Until they need a ride
they leave it locked.

AUTOMATED
found in Roget's Thesaurus #348.25

I am automated woman,
spontaneous,
self-governing, directing,
self-controlled, self-
steered, self-adjusting,
self-closing, self-cocking.
I self-cook, self-dump,
self-empty, self-light,
self-load, self-open, self-prime.
I am self-rising, self-sealing,
self-starting, self-
winding, self-propelled,
semiautomatic,
automanual,
horseless
woman
alone.

COCKTAIL PARTY

He moved his foot, she lit her cigarette,
she lit her cigarette, he moved his foot.
His foot moved, her cigarette lit,
her cigarette, his foot.
He moved, she lit
and no one noticed;
already he knew her touch
and she the star of his need.
Introduced, they spoke,
brief conversation
politely between them,
bubbles floating,
turning, gone.
All night swirled
apart by the party,
careful eyes never met,
never lingered, but
swept each other like beacons.
Someone introduced them again,
and she, keeping
hands to herself
neatly laced,
loosened them only
to reach for the cigarette
he offered.
He moved his foot
and as he moved,
she lit.

ROUNDS

She says Damn him
He comes in taking big strides
in workboots as though he belonged
Hands jammed in his pockets
he settles in the kitchen
by the fire   on the couch
wherever he wants
Then leaves saying
No thanks – have to be someplace
She doesn't believe him
knows he comes for something
and when he's got it he leaves
offering nothing
as though just his presence were enough

She brings him tea with two lumps
because that's how he likes it
She watches every move he makes
foot tapping   drum of fingers
he doesn't say much
She waits for him to turn to her to talk
and when he does she lays herself out before him
her life   her week   her minutes
She knows he comes through just looking
week after week
riding boundaries
checking property
doing rounds

CIRCLE

Ring
I love you
Words I will
never say
Arms around
me, how I
fold into
your life
All that holding
never enough
No beginning
no end
for better
for worse
You there
me here
It could be
a bed
between us:
a room
a whole ocean
this gold
Ring

FEATHERS AND RINGS

She wanders through cities
with feathers wound softly
around her; his arms, his voice
by her side, his words
secret plumes no one hears.
Beside her always, his presence is
solid and real as the fresh round fruit
at the stand on the street –
yellow, golden pears and apples,
smooth moons.

Vegetables call her name,
and on the streets carnations,
heart pink and soul red,
stand tall and close in clear plastic wrap,
gathered tight and secret, waiting
for the exchange of silver,
coins dropped like vows
into vendors hands.
As though someplace
there would be a wedding –

could be a wedding,
vows falling like feathers and rings
through her mind:
feathers, light, airy,
soon enough to blow away;
rings, round, golden, forever,
heavy and timeless as night,
burning wild
through the darkest part
of each pale, tenuous day.

FENCES

Like me, my old horse breaks fence
will not be shut in, no matter how big the field,
but prefers to wander loose
and follow her nose
looking always for new green.

No one knows where she runs
nor the places she stops
to feel the wind and
take in sun.

Sometimes wild-eyed, she gallops up the hill
as though leaving forever;
but always, finally, she bends back home
to the old familiar stall,
the same sweet hay.

SNOW

Pillowed
in this dream
I let go the bed
the house
rise above the field
higher than
buildings or
trees.

I leave my life
a series of
distant lights
sprinkled
pin points
stars.

In the whirl
of white
driven by wind
through air
spinning up
then down
in long even
strokes

smoothly, smoothly
I am
the lightest
touch
the perfect
gesture.

In a gust
spewing
the explosion
blinding
whites out
all else.

This moment
is forever
before
the long slow
ride
returning

to stars
pin points
sprinkled
lights
my life
the bed

this pillow.

BLOSSOM

In my hands this
flower comes to life
as though I were the sun
luring the blossom out,
urging it hour by hour,
minute by minute, open.

The ash pink rose,
closed at first,
shows deep blue-purple veins
like rivers
bringing life
to the tip in tiny dark streams
from the source.

Petals of soft
skin folded darkly
in tiny wrinkles,
too many to count,
slowly uncurl
as creases smooth
and one by one edges
draw back revealing
deep flame.

A slow, swelling song
rises from the root
as sap through the stem
threads liquid crystal,

beading
pure silver
on my finger tip.

INNUENDO

Even over the phone there is
the possibility never stated,
the sweet distant flash that burns connection,
the quickening barely percieved,
a change of cadence, the slightly heightened rhythm
and ring of words; the sweet silences between them
as the image unfolds, the breath is drawn,
and the mind grasps what the body cannot–
the firey dream.   Invention.

Words unwind from dark unspoken places,
feather across the lines we have
all these careful years drawn;
to climb and spiral, stretch
to a distant light never imagined.
Words, tactile, sinuous, almost oily hot to touch,
glisten; they slip between the fingers, yearning,
the scent of them stirs.

Colours from aubergine to orange,
azure strokes and deep red caress and tingle,
and I hear very clearly the loon's
longing, the silvery call over water by night.
I feel moonlight crisp as fresh linen slip over me.
Realization, the flush of heat, the pulse enthralls.
I finger metaphors, and tongue a starry dimension
of wild intent, where anything
is possible, where nothing matters except, except....
Words sift and glitter, dust motes in the mind.

And all at once all the yesterdays and tomorrows,
the once was, should have, could have been, maybes –
those impalpable threads that snare us – snap!
Flung free for an instant, we are brilliance, focus,
the clarity of pure concentrated thought,
the utter simplicity of this sudden deep penetration,
this energy wild between two worlds,
one precise moment, the deepest center.

This word-wrap, word-plunge, word-pump,
word-hammer, word-fire exploding
sudden shivery hot light
in unfathomable darkness
fills, for a moment at least,
the hollow of the heart.

This lightning connection, brief
as one deep breath drawn between two minds,
this union spans all space and silences clocks.
It is the only deep sweet song, of now,
of now, of life that I know.
I hang up the phone and wonder
why not?

IN THE END

Are you like this wine I drink
glass by glass, draining the bottle down?
Shall I savor you slowly,
drink you in, breathing deeply,
the bouquet rolling over my tongue,
tingling fingertips,
weighing me down –
so that by the time you run out
I will be weary,
so weary of the strong rich taste
on my tongue, behind my eyes
the glow hanging heavy as clouds,
thick lids tugging down,
my hands grown slow, clumsy,
tired of all this holding, and
the quickening again and again
like distant thunder's roll;
then sleeping, will I slowly spin you
to a dream that fades
to smooth velvet darkness
where lightning has been,
fades and by morning is gone?

TONIGHT

Tonight I saw a man who looked like you,
how your hair grows, shapes the head,
eyebrows framing eyes
and something in me sprang loose
with feathers and wings.

After all this time
I thought I was over that.
But when he looked at me his eyes showed
no spark, just passing interest,
and my wings folded back to themselves.

I have never been with you
where you did not seek me out
at least with your eyes darkly holding mine;
across rooms, down halls, spanning weeks,
oceans, oh great distance.

In dim light I watched him side-view,
his face perhaps more beautiful than yours,
jaw firmer, cheeks more chisled;
but his face could not stir me on its own.

It was you I saw
who set me free-wheeling
burning into blue,
my secret
wild
revel
alone.

LILACS

Today
there are lilacs in every room,
purple, orchid, tiny pods bursting
pink and mauve light,
and this morning you
filled me with your own sweet seed,
more than I could hold:
ivory, pearls, moonstones, opals.
The scent of you lingers still,
the way, year after year, clusters
of tiny gemstones on slender stems
float amid leafy hearts
and fill whole afternoons of air and sun
with the rich, sticky scent
you can walk through and breathe,
can almost taste,
or feel on your fingers, gleaming silver
(a gathering of secrets and small whispers
deep enough to drown in);
the whole day thick with blossom
pressing down, filling, lifting,
floating, one pure note
rising, a song flying,
breathing again,
a whole chorus of
lilacs.

LIKE DAWN

In shades of soft touches,
flickers of light,
you wake me –
your breath on my neck,
eyelashes brushing;
across my face, hair, and
everywhere the feathery
touch of hands.

Up from darkness
your face on the pillow
glows like a moon, eyes open;
while from the shadows a chair
stirs to life,
each spindle hand-turned.

The table's polished top
gathers whispers,
and from the wall
the mirror's
smooth silvery face
keeps witness,
asks us
nothing.

Slowly, like an eye,
the room opens
as the night's soft flannel
slips off, showing
crisp linen
and pale silk –

a new day.
Outside, leaves
hold silent celebration –
exploding yellow, orange, gold.
Gradually,
gradually like this day,

you enter
and fill me
with new light.

ABOUT THE AUTHOR

The American poet Carol Burnes has gained international recognition for her poetry, performance and teaching. She works as a consultant in creative expression, and workshop leader at a variety of universites, conferences and schools on both sides of the Atlantic. She has performed her work widely, making radio and TV appearances as well. Her first book of poems, <u>Roots and Wings,</u> was published in the US.

Her home is in Weston, MA where her family has lived for four generations, and the New England roots go deep. She lives in a converted barn, down a long dirt road, with her husband, has two children, and a menagerie of creatures whom she esteems as much for their complex personalities as for their feathers and fur.